ONE WONDERFUL YOU
by
Francie Portnoy

a unique book for adopted people of all ages

Published by
The Children's Home Society of North Carolina

One Wonderful You

© 1997 by Francie Portnoy
Published by The Children's Home Society of North Carolina
Printed in the United States of America

SUMMARY: An explanation of how adoptees are a wonderful blend of two families.

ISBN 0-9643051-1-9
[1. Adoption - Juvenile literature.] I. Higgs, Tracy, ill. II. Title

for my two families

my father, Harry Portnoy
and in loving memory of my mother, Becky Portnoy

my birthmother, Judith Barry
my birthfather, Robert Conley

You are unique.

(Go look it up in the dictionary.)

Unique: yōo nēk, a. single in kind; having no like or equal; unusual; different.

Now don't go getting a swelled head about it
Everyone is unique.

Some people are unique,
or different,
because they are
very,
very
tall.

Some because they
wear their hair in an
unusual style.

Others are unique because
they can play a violin so beautifully.

Or maybe they can build long, high bridges.

I guess you
could say that
everyone is
unique in her
(or his)
own way.

One of the ways you are unique
is that you were adopted.

Do you know what that really means?

Well, one thing it doesn't mean is that you were "chosen." Years ago some people would say that what made adopted children so special (just another word for unique) was that they were "chosen," kind of like your mom and dad went to a Baby Department Store and walked up and down the aisle looking for just the right child.

Have you ever seen a Baby Department Store?

Highly unlikely!

Most likely what really happened is that a couple (a man and a woman) came together and made a baby - you. They were your birthmother and birthfather. Your birthmother carried you in her womb (a special place near her tummy) for nine whole months.

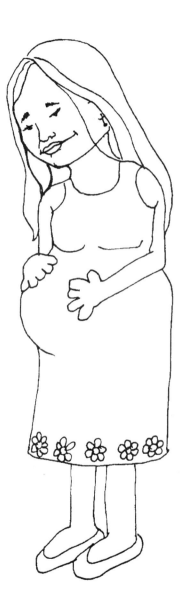

During that time, you grew and grew and grew. When you were ready, you were born (probably at a hospital, just like most other babies).

For some reason your birthmother and birthfather couldn't give a child all the things a child needs. They couldn't parent you.

All children need someone who can parent them. Someone who is able to feed them, change them, hold them, play with them, teach them, keep them safe, take them to pre-school and dance lessons and baseball, buy them clothes, take them to the doctor . . .

Phew! This parenting stuff is hard!

Luckily, there were people (sometimes one person) who were able to be parents. And they very much wanted to have a child. Somehow the connection was made. Either an agency, a lawyer, a doctor,

a friend or a family member knew about a child (YOU) who needed parents. They also knew about someone (a couple or a single person) who wanted to parent a child. That is probably how your adoptive parents came to be your PARENTS.

And that is how you all became a family.

ow this is where your being adopted makes
u unique. You are unique because you are a
onderful blend of two families - your birth
mily and your adoptive family. You are
nique because it took <u>two</u> families to make
e you.

"Two families?"

Yes, you are a blend of two families.

Your birth family, because you were born to them, gave you certain things.

Your beautiful eyes came from your birth family.

So did your dark,
curly hair.

Those big feet, too, must run in your birth family somewhere.

All of these things are "genetic" traits that you got from your birth family.

But did you know that you also got much of your personality from your birth family?

Well, you did!

Whether you are outgoing,

or more of the quiet type,

has a lot to do with genetics.

So you probably got many of your personality traits from your birth family.

Are you creative?

Do you prefer to follow the crowd?

Are you orderly?

Or are you more comfortable with casual (some may say messy) living?

Are you shy,

or the life of the party?

These traits were given to you at birth - they came from your birth parents.

'But doesn't everybody get those things from the parents they were born to?"

Yes!

"So what makes me unique then?"

(I just knew you were smart!!)

What makes you unique is that, yes, you were born with certain genetic traits, just like all kids are. But then you were adopted into another family, and from then on that family had a lot to do with helping you become who you are.

Your adoptive family probably gave you your name.

They gave you your home, the city and state you live in, and much of your identity (the way you describe yourself).

You probably got your religion from your adoptive family.

Family traditions

and family memories came from your adoptive family.

Your pets
are also part of
your adoptive family.

And you got aunts, uncles,

cousins, and grandparents.

Your adoptive family has also helped you develop your particular talents and tastes

by encouraging you to take part in many different experiences.

You are who you are because of all the wonderful things you were born with (from your birth family) and because of all the great stuff your adoptive family gave you.